*hand
in
hand*

hand in hand

poems from
being present
at the end of life

Mimi S Dupont

Hand in Hand: Poems From Being Present at the End of Life
Copyright © 2025 Mimi S Dupont

ISBN: 979-8-218-65063-6

First Edition

All Rights Reserved. No part of this book may be reproduced in any form or by an electronic or mechanical means, including information storage and retrieval systems without permission in writing from the publisher, except by a reviewer who may quote brief passages in a review. For information, address mimidupontstories@gmail.com.

Cover & Interior Design/Layout and
Publishing assistance provided by:
Crystal Heidel, Heimat Publishing

Cover Image from Unsplash.com, provided by the British Library, published on February 19, 2020; Image taken from page 95 of *Flowers of Song. A choice selection from the poets, with illustrations and an introduction* by F. E. Weatherly.

Printed in the USA

hand in hand

A WORD BEFORE YOU READ THESE POEMS

I wrote these poems without pain, without
struggle, without fear, without
hesitation. The words emerged from,
poured out of, or sprouted from
the silence and stillness in me that resulted from
attending someone's death.
Someone. Some One.

Almost 9,000 people die every day in the U.S.
'People' is plural. But every one of that large
number is one, one person, one individual,
someone's father, mother, sister, brother,
spouse, lover, enemy, friend,
boss, coworker, neighbor, child.

How comfortable are you around someone
who is dying? Are you silent because
you don't know what to say? Are you afraid
you'll say or do something wrong? Something
foolish? Something hurtful?
Do you feel edgy? Do you squirm at the thought
of going into a hospital room,
a hospice room?

Most people in our culture do.
We can feel awkward or afraid
around people who are dying.
It's a place where our standard "How are you?"
doesn't work.

A friend recently told me
of her experience at
a meditation gathering the previous night.
The leader mentioned how compassion can be
hard when you don't know what to say.
My friend shared a conversation she and I
had when her son-in-law died.
I'd called her and said something
comforting. I didn't remember it.
But my friend did.

She said that when her mother
died, she didn't remember anything
anyone had said. It was their presence
that mattered. "I remember you called me and said
'We can both speak, you can speak and
I will just listen, or we can
both be on the phone in silence'.
THAT was compassion."

I tell this story because once in a while
we all get it right, even when we don't feel
confident in our expressions of compassion.

We know better than to tell a grieving
parent they can have another baby
or console a sad pet owner
with a question about getting a new
cat or dog.

Every creature that comes into being
on this planet is unique, takes its place in this
physical world, in this time and space,
lives in relationship.

I noticed early in my adult life that I
experienced a different emotional state
around individuals who were gravely
ill or dying. While others seemed to be
visibly upset — crying, wringing their hands,
jabbering or unable to speak — I felt a
deep sense of peace, a silence, a stillness that
enabled me to speak calmly and quietly to those
around me. I saw that this was comforting to them.

That led me to serve as a hospice vigil volunteer,
someone who is present with a person who is
actively dying.

My purpose here is simply to share some
of my experiences around people who are dying
in the hope you may become a bit more comfortable.

When we're comfortable enough to talk with
someone who is dying, or just be with them
there is so much more to experience
during that time with
a person we love.

DISAGREEMENT

Well, kids, I'll tell you
After sinking my shoulder into the depths
of the hospitable loveseat
so as to nestle against
and hold the hand of
a frail, forgetful old woman
whose husband died at thirty-nine
whose only son died at twenty
and whose only daughter was going to die momentarily
before her eyes
so as to listen to her side of the disagreement
I'll tell you what she said

She said she wanted the priest
and the church and the burial
and the whole thing the way it was done
for her husband first and then her son

This lonely and brokenhearted woman
disagreed with her daughter's long-time lover
the significant other who
said, oh so quietly, like the kind of man he was
and so very respectfully
recognizing her sadness
that her daughter told him she wanted none of
her mother's ways of
going out

finishing up
ending her days
that her daughter told him she wanted to be cremated
and to spread her ashes on the ocean

I don't know what they decided

But, kids, I'll tell you
Do what you want with me when my spirit departs
I don't care

BREAKFAST

What does a poet eat for breakfast?

    At 7:37 a.m. today

My gurgling belly wants that banana on the counter
peeled, revealed, its tender flesh bruised
beyond redemption. In an unceremonious burial
it goes into the garbage with the coffee grounds

    my friend texted her sadness

My memory wants nothing for breakfast
It remains full from Saturday's lunchtime gathering
of the Fancy Broads and conversation about
our sadnesses and joys, fears and frustrations:
Linda's lingering sadness over her mother's death
which brought us together two days ago
and her son's death — he who
had named us, at nine, because we dressed in our best
whenever we convened; Barbara's joy
at a long-awaited retirement date still in the future
but firm and full of food for her
dreams; my fear that I will not be able to make
the music that feeds me once my hand is
surgically repaired; our friend's frustration with
the details swirling around as her
mother teetered on the brink of recovery or death

    "All: my mother died this morning. Thanks for your support."

My heart wants to know the choices to break fast
Nothing for you today, Dear Heart
Perhaps tomorrow
Fasting will cleanse you

I am starving
even for words

My soul will eat poems for breakfast

DEATH | MINE

I will die in a daughter's nondescript guest room
in a rented hospital bed
on a blustery autumn day
sometime after my eighty-eighth birthday

Another daughter will attend to my nursing needs
although she has not been a practicing nurse
for many years now and the third daughter
will be concentrating on what loss means
this time
in this place
as she begins to make arrangements
for what will happen once my spirit has departed
its confinement

That's the daughter I told years ago to
just burn my body to a fine ash
and distribute it in their gardens
these three daughters and my son

And those four will say
Mimi has died
no one but them knowing
that the IRS and DMV know me
by another name

Come spring my ashes will be
dispersed like seed in the wind
among four gardens
and my headstone
will be a short stick
among the others
Radishes, Spinach, Lettuce, Mimi

LAST BREATH

When I awoke this morning
the square on my calendar for today was blank
By the time I finished drinking my coffee
hospice called and asked if I might be able
to stay for an hour or two
with a man whose wife wanted
to run home for a change of clothes
"Sure," I said. "I can be there in forty-five minutes."

Although I was late she said
thanks and left quickly

I took her husband's warm hand
from under the white-on-white woven blanket
kept from weighing on his feet
by the yellowing foam which
raised the edges of his bed

He was nonresponsive
which means he did not acknowledge that I said
he was surrounded by love
he was safe
he could depart when he was ready

He left, departed, died
forty-five minutes after his wife went out the door
The hospice nurse was in the room with me
We agreed the breath we saw together was his last

She went out to tell the staff
They called the wife who, remember,
only went home to get a change of clothes
so she could stay with him the night

I was afraid she would be angry at me
for being there without her when he died

When she walked back through the door
she went straight to his bed
put her hands tenderly on the sides of his face
said "Now you can finally rest."

Then she looked up at me
"Well, he definitely didn't want me here."

HOW TO COMFORT AROUND DEATH

8:45 a.m. on a warm spring day
Reach for the phone which is singing
from the far bedside table
Look to see who is calling
Remember how kind and cheerful
the hospice volunteer coordinator always is
when she calls to ask you to sit with someone
who is imminent, someone who is about to die
Choose to answer the call
Say yes, yes, you have time
today is your unscheduled day
He should not be alone just because his family is away
Say you can be there in sixty minutes

Shower. Dress
presentable this time
since you are going out
since you are representing hospice
Chastise yourself for taking longer to prepare
than you think you should while someone is dying

9:16 a.m. Call back the volunteer coordinator
for the details. Write down his name, his
patient number, which facility, what room number, his
diagnosis, why he is alone
Get your hospice bag with your ID badge
pen and prayer book from the closet
Check that it contains a water bottle or two

Wonder how long you will be there
Wonder if you should take time for breakfast
Wonder if you should call the diner and
pick up breakfast and eat it on the way
balancing the open styrofoam square between
the steering wheel and your chest
Choose against breakfast
Add a banana to the hospice bag
Grab the bag, the purse, the keys, the
rose-colored corduroy shirt hanging by the door
in case his room is cold. Or you are

Let go of arranging

Back out of the driveway
Turn on the radio. Hear it
but don't listen to it because you
are anxious about getting there quickly
Drive attentively

Decide to drive through the Dunkin Donuts
for coffee to go. Chastise yourself for taking
four minutes off task while someone is dying
Comfort yourself that you've had no coffee
no breakfast and you have no idea
how long you will be there

10:01 a.m. Sign in at the facility desk
Write 10:00 under "in" because
it will be easier to calculate the time for
hospice records when you call the
automated answering service to report the
information for this assignment
so hospice can report to Medicare
Ride the elevator up
Ask at the nurses' station where his room is
Follow the nurse passing behind you
who says she will show you
Listen on the way down the hall
to the nurse who says a friend is with him
Realize you are surprised because you thought
he would be alone, unattended
Approach the room quietly
See the visitor's back as she sits next to his bed
Listen as the visitor turns and says to the nurse
"I think he just passed."
His sallow color says she is right

Chastise yourself again for getting coffee
Know that if you had not
you would have been here when he died

Let go of the guilt

Wonder why people are always saying
"passed" when die is what we do

Let go of the judgment

Stand in silence on the opposite side of the bed
Touch his arm, his face. Hold his lifeless hand
After a time ask the visitor how she knew him
Listen. Learn that she is his neighbor
Was. Was his neighbor. Learn that she is
a friend of his brother who was here last week
from his home in another state. Learn
that he has two sons who live in the Midwest

Step aside as the nurse returns with
her stethoscope to verify his death
Step aside so the visitor can remain seated
her hand resting gently on his mottled arm
Stand quietly as the nurse says she must
listen for two minutes. Watch as
the seated visitor fumbles for the switch
as instructed and turns off the oxygen machine
Hear the silence. Watch as the nurse feels for
the pulse that is not there. Watch her as
she walks toward the door. Listen as
she says she will call the family
and call hospice with her nurse's report

Walk over and touch him again
his hand, his arm, his face. Look up
as someone enters the room, someone
who is crying. She says "Oh, I'm too late."

Step away from the bed and linger
by the wall. Notice the photo of him with
someone older who looks of Asian descent
Listen as these two visitors, these women
who know him — knew him — but not each other
begin to speak. Listen as their words dance
awkwardly through the introductions
Listen as one says she lives — lived — down the street from him
from his house, and she knew his family lived
elsewhere so she came. Listen to her voice break
as she says "I thought someone should be here."
Remember your surprise that you and he would not
be alone. Realize you are grateful that
you and he are not alone

Listen as the second woman says she has been
his friend for 40 years. Listen as she says they go
to dinner maybe once a month. Went. Went to dinner
Realize she will have no more dinners with him
Listen as she cries. Reach out as she moves
sideways toward you still looking at his face
and let her slip into your open arm
Put your other hand on her hand

Listen as she expresses her gratitude to
the first visitor that she was here when he died
Notice she does not say "died"
Listen as she laments again that she was
not here in time. Reassure her that he knew
he knew she was coming
he knew he was loved. Listen
as silence spreads through the room like
a woman's perfume
Four people
Three hearts beating

Notice the nurse returning
"What happens now?" the second visitor asks
"We'll collect his things," she begins
The first visitor says she is his neighbor and
can take his belongings if that is okay
The second visitor says she can take his
clothes to the thrift shop since
no family lives nearby
No one will want his clothes
The nurse says she will get some plastic bags
adding they have only trash bags
Notice that her voice holds no guilt about
the coldness of trash bags, only regret

Help the others collect what came
into the room with him
Take the two small pictures off the wall where they hang
far apart on nails clearly meant for
something else. Remember the second visitor told you
the Asian woman, Chinese in fact, is his mother
She said his grandmother was Russian
Notice he looks nothing like her
Hand the framed photographs to the first visitor
who has collected the other photos and
thinking-of-you cards from the windowsill
Notice how dusty and faded the cards
and empty envelopes seem now that the person
for whom they were intended is lifeless

Help put into a trash bag the clean clothes
destined for someone else's use
Put the dirty clothes in a trash bag
Knot it closed and deposit it by the trash can
Clear the bathroom vanity of his toiletries
Unplug the electric toothbrush and place it
gently in the trash can

Notice the first visitor preparing to leave
Listen to her say goodbye to him
Realize you don't remember when she
disclosed that she is a nurse, or was
and that she is a hospice volunteer, but
not here. Not now. She fills neither of those roles
today. Listen as she reminds herself she is here
as a friend. Watch her sad eyes turn away

See the nurse return with a rolling cart
so the second visitor can more easily take
to her car the bags of clothes
Help load the bags into the cart
Ask her about the small oval vase of
faded rose blooms. "I'll take those even though
they are already dead." Tell her she can finish drying
the blossoms and tie a ribbon around them
Notice the brown along the edges of the palest possible pink
Wonder if the roses had really been white

Take the elevator down with the second visitor
and her cart, a young man with a guitar, and
a staff person wheeling a woman with
a long thin gray ponytail

11:03 a.m. Sign out yourself and the second visitor
Help her load the bags into her car
Take the cart back inside. Drive away

Notice the depth of the silence within you as if
you have brought the silence with you from his room
Do not speak. Do not let out of you
any of what you have seen and heard
Drive toward home

Do not stop to do errands
Let go of your effort toward efficiency
Do not stop to see the friends whose house
you will pass, whom you have promised a hundred times
to visit. Let go of the guilt about broken promises

Wonder if you give the dying better treatment than the living

Keep driving. Drive home in silence
Do not speak. Do not even open
your mouth and let out the hollow stillness inside you
Do not let out the silence you brought from his room
Keep it. Contain it

Pull into the driveway
Carry in the hospice bag, the purse, the keys
the rosy corduroy shirt. Put them away
Watch the time on the phone flip from 11:59 to 12:00
Walk upstairs to the kitchen
Wash the antiseptic smell off your hands
Dry them. Step out into the
sunshine on the small wooden deck by
your kitchen. Notice the spring green of
the leaves on the tree by the railing
Inhale new life

Let it all go

MARY'S DEATH

I knew Mary
for three hours and thirteen minutes
or thereabouts
during which
she labored through her last breaths
while her husband
in his black plaid shirt
cried his eyes out
cried his heart out
cried out
again and again
that he did not know how to do this
but he leaned over anyway
and passed on the kiss
that came through the phone
from a friend

I listened to him
and to his mother
locked inside her Alzheimer's mind
who said little
and to his father
in his red plaid shirt
who said a lot
about what the Bible says
and I considered
what I should reply
But I was there to listen after all

So I said little
and listened a lot
especially to the recorded messages
of her raspy voice
that her husband had already preserved

I'd never been asked to listen
to a voice mail before
while we waited for someone to die
But after her husband
fumbled with the buttons on the phone
getting through remotely
to their home answering machine
he said he'd like me to listen
to her last few messages
if I wouldn't mind
and I said I did not mind one bit
So he handed me the receiver
with the curly cord attached
and I listened to her voice then
her throaty last-few-days voice
in which she asked him
tenderly
to bring her a shirt and jeans

I listened to the message
in which she said
she missed him
and the message
in which she sang him happy birthday
from her hospital bed

Then I put the phone back in its cradle
and turned to Mary and held her hand
and what I said I do not remember
but I heard her husband's father say
"now there is witness"
and I said goodbye
and went down the hall

In the lobby I saw
a person I know
the kind of person who makes everyone else's job
not easier maybe
but full of heart
full of gratitude
full of love
that flows in and out of rooms
and in and out of eyes and across hands
and into hearts
and lets us
let others go

And as we parted
she and I
Mary's husband's father
came down the hall and said
with half a breath
"I think we've lost her"
and signaled for me to come back
So I did
and I don't remember what happened then
Isn't that the way
when our hearts are so full
they empty through our eyes
and hands and exhalations
and then there is silence
except for the sobs

HOW LONG?

LOSS
Noun
1 *detriment or disadvantage from failure*
to get something or keep it; **2** *deprived of*
or without something one has had; **3** *death,*
loss of a loved one

Sometimes loss is minor —
misplaced keys, a middle school sporting match,
a lottery ticket that didn't pay out. We can deny or
rationalize or discard as temporary these
discomforts. But death? That's a permanent loss
Still, the word itself — loss — doesn't describe
the vast emptiness, the airless void inside us
somewhere between our lungs and diaphragms
the sensation of nothingness as we inhale and exhale
feeling not the life-giving air
unaware even that we are breathing

When we lose a loved one to death's finality
sometimes the shock bores into us more deeply
than we expect. Perhaps we are stricken by a death
seemingly outside what we see as our emotional circle
Perhaps we will not know for a long time why
the sense of loss stays with us, haunts us, shadows us
Perhaps we will never know
why we are touched so deeply

I was shaken in such a way
by the death of a childhood friend
during our young adulthood
We grew up in the same suburb
went to the same Catholic grade school
and the same small girls-only Catholic
high school that our mothers attended
We were friends but not the kind who stay on
the phone each night confiding innermost longings
and hopes, disappointments and dreams. After
rescheduling our 20-year high school reunion to
spring because she had breast cancer and might not
live until the original autumn date
she died anyway a few weeks before the event

One reaction to death
is anger. Anger that we've been abandoned
left behind, inconvenienced, deprived
Many of us who had graduated together
gathered at her funeral
sad ourselves as we consoled
her husband and two children then eight and ten
whom most of us did not know
I felt helpless, useless

In the few weeks between the funeral and reunion
I didn't understand why the death of a person I had not
seen but once or twice in the previous twenty years
would profoundly alter my view of life
and death. Maybe I was shaken because she was
so young and I felt afraid that might happen to me, too
dying young
Maybe I was haunted because her children were
not much older than mine then aged seven, five and two
Maybe I was shocked because I was pregnant
and she was dead
My possibilities endless
Hers gone

I think my schoolmate's death at thirty-seven stunned me so much
because it was the first
the first death I'd experienced as an adult
the first time mortality had mocked my flimsy film of denial
the first time a crack appeared in my youthful sense of
immunity to harm

But loss is just a word
the condition of not having something
or someone
which is gone

Last Sunday night when my cousin's wife
told me by phone she didn't think my cousin
was going to make it
out of the hospital alive
I said I would be there the next day
hung up
turned out the lights
and lit a candle

As millions watched an awards show
animating their smart TVs
I watched the flicker of a single flame
reflected in the matte black screen
One candle, lit, can banish darkness

I watched as the crimson wax
dripped down itself and
drop by drop landed
on the lip of the irreparably tarnished
brass candlestick

I sat on my sofa alone
under a tent of darkness
illuminated by a single flame
one candle between me and utter blindness
dependent on light to see

I watched as the flame which
enveloped all but the base of the wick
hunkered down close to the bowl of
melted wax atop the taper
or stretched up
far beyond the wick's tip
fed by some rivulet of oxygen in the nearby air
either dancing
or still

I was brave enough to whisk my finger through
the elongated flame
seeking momentary pain
but not brave enough to lick my thumb and forefinger
and douse the flame with my own saliva
What is 'brave enough'?

Loss
How long will we feel it?
Forever?

WHAT I KEPT
After Irene Fick's *What We Keep*

This is what I kept
from the experience of watching my cousin die
from the death that meant
she would no longer be available by phone
by email, by conversation over coffee together
in deeply cushioned chairs on a front porch in Maine
on a warm and foggy August morning
I kept her courage and perseverance
as she faced a life of continuous struggles
all of which she overcame except
the final challenge
the one none of us can win

On that August trip
she climbed a series of stairways
to a lighthouse at the top of a rocky point
her oxygen pack over her shoulder
She looked up to the top
looked down at her feet
and set out step by step

I have kept the image of my cousin
climbing toward the light
In August she made it to the top
By January she was gone

ALMOST

I sit with patients who are actively dying
which seems like a contradiction in terms
but 'actively dying' means death is imminent
almost dead

I've stayed into the darkest part of the night with a woman
whose significant other did not know I live around the corner from him
nor did I tell him so before he left for the night
during which I accompanied her to her final breath

I've stayed with a woman
whose husband cried when she died
after which I went home and pried open
a plastic container of guacamole
ate it with some crackers
never tasting any of it
not one bit

I've stayed ... well ... last night
I stayed with a woman whose niece
needed some space, some time
to clear the tear stains from her face

Every night she'd expected to be called
she told me
at some moment in the early morning darkness
but the call had not yet come
I do not know if last night was the night she was called

I left after five hours of holding her unresponsive aunt's hand
and being
just being with her

Holding her hand as the sunlight waned
and the inky blackness pasted itself
to the far side of the windowpanes
I knew we were both almost
there. Almost where?

It's been said we are all dying
from birth onwards so
when I left last night
I was reminded again
that we are all
every one of us
almost done
almost gone
almost home

DUST

I hate to dust
In fact, I hate dust
It reminds me of mortality

Christians gather on what
is affectionately known as 'Ash' Wednesday
to begin a period of penitence before Easter
A cross of ash is marked on foreheads
and solemn words spoken, invoking Adam
the so-called first man
Remember, Man, that thou art dust
and unto dust thou shalt return

But humans also contain water
Newborns are about three-quarters water
By age one that drops to sixty-five percent
and settles in
at fifty to sixty-five percent in adults
Muscle contains seventy-five percent water
body fat only ten percent

Okay, we're made of dust and water
You know what dust and water make when
you mix them?
Mud
So apparently in humans
dust and water have a close encounter but
a near miss, since none of us ends up
eventually as a mud puddle

A scientist in an Air Force study of UFO's in the fifties and sixties
developed a 'close encounter classification system'
A close encounter of the first kind is seeing a UFO
the second is physical evidence an alien exists
and the third is actual contact with alien life forms

I wonder if dust is an alien life form

A *New York Times* story said scientists have seen
cosmic dust in a galaxy far, far away
The light has been on its way for thirteen-point-two billion years
I guess dust existed before much else
certainly before Adam

Abraham of the Old Testament called himself
'dust and ashes'
dust being earth or other matter
in fine dry particles or a cloud of same
ash the powdery residue that remains after burning
like from a crematorium
or a seriously seared marshmallow from a campfire

I would rather encounter an alien
than reside eternally in an urn
on someone's mantel
or be dusted off the dresser

OVER AND OVER

This month I've been down a road
I used to love
because it took me where I wanted to go
to the beach or
to the small towns I like to explore
or to the splintery old wooden ferry boat
that crossed an Eastern Shore river
a ferry I started riding 45 years ago
when I was in college
my squirmy gut settling at the sight of
the other landing across the river

But I've been down that long road so
many times this month
that I'm tired

I drove that route to see my cousin
in a comfortable hospital room when
after she consumed chocolate ice cream
a Diet Coke and the remains of a milkshake
in half an hour I thought
she was going to recover
I drove that route again to watch her
struggle unsuccessfully for breath

I drove that route to help plan her memorial service
and again to attend that service at which
two others and I shared our reflections
amid the midwinter daisies and yellow roses

I drove that route to Washington a week later
for a happy brunch and theater outing
after which I hit a pothole that ripped open my
expensive run-flat tire

That's why I'm tired

The death of my cousin
The death of my tire

I can replace the tire

TODAY

Pardon my late posting
in our daily poetry challenge
but I have been busy today

I thought it would be an ordinary day

I woke to an empty square on
the calendar my friend gave me
with her extraordinary photos of our world

I have attended two deaths this afternoon
two
and I am tired

I was just finishing my coffee when
I answered the hospice call
a last-minute yes
for a woman who just needed to run home
for a change of clothes so she could stay the night
with her husband who
died while she was gone
I held his hand and did not
let go until she returned during which time
his mottled purple hand faded to yellow

Then I left for a friend's house whose
mother was dying
her mother also a friend
and as I entered every person looked
up at me and one said
"She's gone."

I stopped there where
my feet were planted on the floor and

well, there is much more to tell
but I am tired
and this day is over and

I fear I have not risen to the occasion

well, not risen to the day's poetry challenge
but surely risen to the compassion challenge
I am tired and . . . well . . .

this shall be a poem someday soon

Good night

ACKNOWLEDGMENTS

Many thanks to Judy Catterton and Ellen Collins for their editing suggestions, and to Crystal Heidel for leading me through the publishing process.

ABOUT THE AUTHOR

Mimi S Dupont, EdD, spent years writing reportage and features for newspapers, organizational documents, state and national grant proposals, parent notes to teachers, and a dissertation. She now writes poetry, personal essays, other creative nonfiction, and is working on a novel. She lives halfway between a small town in coastal Delaware and the eastern edge of the continent.

www.ingramcontent.com/pod-product-compliance
Lightning Source LLC
Chambersburg PA
CBHW051704040426
42446CB00009B/1292